THE MESSENGER'S COMPANION

THE MESSENGER'S COMPANION

A QUICK GUIDE TO EASILY PREPARE IMPACTFUL 20-MINUTE DEVOTIONS

MIKE KASTLE

Tall Pine

"Also I heard the voice of the Lord, saying:

'Whom shall I send,
And who will go for Us?'
Then I said, 'Here am I! Send me.'"

(Isaiah 6:8 NKJV)

DEDICATION

To Ermao, my good friend and brother overseas, a true messenger of the Lord. Your life and your words magnificently communicate the gospel message, which has touched so many in Asia, and me. May God bless you and multiply the open doors before you to share His heart, and yours, with the many, many who still are unreached.

CONTENTS

PART 1
STRESS FREE PREPARATION

> Sing to the Lord, bless His name. Proclaim the good news
> of His salvation from day to day. Declare His glory among
> the nations, His wonders among all peoples. (Psalm 96:2-3)

DEVOTIONAL MESSAGES ARE A POSITIVE WAY TO START ANY meeting, whether during a mission trip, church meeting, family gathering, or other times. They provide the opportunity to help the group focus on the Lord and to prepare their hearts for what is ahead.

The purpose of this book is to help you to develop a devotional message so that you can easily and comfortably share it with others. This book is meant to help you organize your thoughts and messages in a way that is personal to you so that you can easily communicate them to your audience.

You may feel that you are not "spiritual" enough to lead a devotion, or that your understanding of the Bible may not be significant enough to deliver an applicable and engaging message. Or, you may just be afraid of public speaking.

Maybe you simply have difficulty organizing your thoughts in a way that you can share, and you could use a little help. This book will help guide you through the process of preparing and sharing your devotion by making it as simple and painless as possible so you can communicate an awesome message!

Many of us, even those who are spiritually mature, may be somewhat shy and fearful of delivering a devotional message in public. I understand this because I used to be the same way. In fact, I remember during my early years as a law student in America, sometimes I would be so fearful that I may be called on by the professor to answer a question during class that I could actually feel the perspiration drip down my arm. I was almost always prepared for each class, but simply the feeling of anticipation that I may be called upon to share publicly felt overwhelming. However, the more I interacted in class (usually against my will), the more comfortable I began to feel in doing it. So too with devotions! The more you lead devotional messages, the more comfortable you will become.

Throughout my career as a lawyer, and my ministry as a team leader and missionary, I have had the privilege of sharing many devotional messages to a wide range of audiences. Sometimes I have had plenty of time to prepare the message, but at times I had to lead the devotional message on a moment's notice. And I've also had the opportunity to ask others to lead devotional messages and coached them through the process. Usually, during a week-long mission trip, I ask a different person each morning to bring a devotional message so that we may begin the day by focusing on the Lord. Sometimes, for whatever reason, the one who had planned to bring the message could not do so. So, I needed to pick up the ball and lead the devotion for the team. So, I've learned that it is good to be prepared, at any time, to share an encouraging word of hope and blessing from the Word of God, to any audience. Second Timothy 4:2 tells us that we should *"be ready in season and out of season. Convince, rebuke, exhort, with all longsuffering and teaching."* Therefore, developing skills to prepare and share a devotional message, without a long preparation period, may be helpful for all of us.

Devotional messages take many different forms. And there are many ways to prepare them and deliver them. There is no "right way" or "wrong way" to do this. Preparing and delivering a devotional message can and should be a VERY flexible process. This Guide offers two main devotional message formats. These are easy-to-use formats that provide a very good and organized way to help you prepare and deliver your devotion with excellence and ease.

Whether you are sharing your devotional message with a mission team, friends, family, or strangers, it is important to organize your message at least one day before you share it. That way, you will have an opportunity to think about it and mentally "digest" what you have prepared in case other ideas come to your mind that help to illustrate your points, and it helps to give you time to make changes to your message before you deliver it.

Sometimes, of course, this may not be possible. On

mission teams, for example, many times unexpected things may happen during a day. So, we may not be able to have adequate preparation time for our message. Although our intent was to set aside quality time to reflect and to prepare a message, in the end, we actually may not have the opportunity to do this. Therefore, I have included twelve good examples of devotional messages I have given during teams or other meetings, so you can immediately pick up any of these and share them with your audience.

Sharing God's Word is one of the greatest privileges on earth. I sincerely hope that this Quick Guide will help you to prepare what the Lord has put on your heart to share with others, and hopefully relieve some stress in the process. May the Lord guide you and bless you richly as you share!

For the word of God is living and powerful, and sharper than any two-edged sword, piercing even to the division of soul and spirit, and of joints and marrow, and is a discerner of the thoughts and intents of the heart. (Hebrews 4:12)

THE PURPOSE OF A DEVOTION IS TO DRAW YOUR AUDIENCE TO connect with Jesus, to hear His word for them for the moment. This may include words of encouragement, exhortation, direction, and/or the gospel message. Therefore, it is helpful to structure your devotion in one of two formats:

1. <u>Biblical Text Devotion Format</u>, which you can use to structure your devotion around a specific Bible verse or passage; or

2. <u>Topical Devotion Format</u>, which you can use to structure your devotional message around a specific topic (which you will then support by

> various scriptural references and discussion
> about each of them).

Either of these two formats are fine to use, and they are both explained in more detail in Chapter 3.

CHOOSING A SCRIPTURE FOR A BIBLICAL TEXT DEVOTION

Choosing the specific biblical text you will use is the first step in delivering your Biblical Text Devotion. Your biblical text can be long or short. It can be direct or it can be a biblical story. Any biblical text is generally fine to use. God's Word is powerful. The Holy Spirit will use His Word to touch hearts and speak what is on His heart to those who hear your message. You will begin your devotional message by reading the text or by asking someone else in the audience to read it.

If you already have a scripture verse or a biblical story on your heart to share, then use it. God places His Word on our hearts and minds for a reason, so it is likely that the Holy Spirit is prompting you to share it. If you are not yet sure if your scripture verse is the one He would like for you to share, you can simply ask Him, and He will show you this and He may instead redirect you to another biblical passage to use.

If you do not already have a scripture verse on your heart to share, simply ask the Lord to show you one. Then, read the Bible prayerfully, particularly those chapters and stories that are most meaningful to you personally. As you read, keep your spiritual ears open and listen to Him as He directs you to those verses that you should use as your biblical text. God speaks to us (and others) through His Word, so you can trust Him to direct you as you read His Word for the verses to share. Remember, the best biblical text to use for your devotional message is the one that you feel God is leading you to share.

CHOOSING A TOPIC FOR A TOPICAL DEVOTION

When choosing a topic for your Topical Devotion, here are some general tips:

- Consider your audience. Don't choose a topic that may be too complicated for the audience you are speaking to. Don't worry if your topic may seem too simple, as the simplest words often have the deepest impact on your audience. God's Word is true and powerful no matter how basic and fundamental it may seem.
- Avoid controversial topics. Leave those for private conversations or blogs, not a public devotion. Your goal is not to preach, but to engage thought and to bring uplifting reflection from the Word of God. So, choose a topic that is meant to bless the hearers and to bring positive insight and change.
- Avoid topics involving discussions of politics, sex, and public affairs where there are differing and conflicting opinions. This is important because a

devotion is meant to open hearts and minds to the Lord so that He can speak to the hearers. It is meant to be uplifting and encouraging. It is not a time to drive home a particular point of view that you may have and of which you may wish to convince others.

- Avoid topics that could involve major differing interpretations of scripture by your particular audience. If we choose topics with multiple possible interpretations of scripture, your devotion may devolve into a discussion of doctrine rather than a message of life to connect your hearers to the Lord. This is especially true if we use scripture verses that have different interpretations based upon a different translation of the Bible.

Finally, if you are still unsure about a particular Biblical Text or a Topic for your message, you can always use any of the 12 *Usable Examples* in this book.

3 / PREPARE YOUR DEVOTION
(EASY PROCESS)

The preparations of the heart belong to man, But the answer of the tongue is from the Lord. (Proverbs 16:1)

IT IS NOT NECESSARY TO WRITE OUT YOUR WHOLE DEVOTION ON paper. Instead, I recommend that you simply prepare a handwritten outline of your message that you can use to guide you as you speak, using one of the two structural formats below.

As you prepare your handwritten outline, I encourage you to do this on a one-fourth page or one-half page of "Letter size" or "A4 size" paper. Using a one-fourth size page makes it easy for you to hold, while still being able to read the outline as you share. This also helps you to keep the outline small enough so that you do not have too many points and thus drag out the devotion longer than it should be. So, I recommend that you take a sheet of paper, fold it in half, and then fold it in half again. This will give you a one-fourth size page to use. If your handwritten outline must be longer, you can always let your notes overflow onto the back of the page.

Here is how to prepare your devotion and devotion notes for both the Biblical Text Devotion format and the Topical Devotion format. You can be flexible and deviate from these formats as you wish. This is meant to simply provide an easy framework for you to use, not a rigid requirement.

BIBLICAL TEXT DEVOTION FORMAT

The Biblical Text Devotion format has 4 simple parts. You can add additional parts to your devotion if you wish. However, this four-part structure is simple and adequate for a great devotional message:

- Bible Text
- Observations of the verse(s)
- Application of the verse(s)
- Closing

Here is a more detailed description of what you will write under each of these headings on your Biblical Text Devotion handwritten outline. You can make an outline of your own devotion from the biblical text you have chosen, or you may simply use one of the Biblical Text Devotion Examples I have prepared in chapters 5-12 of this book.

BIBLE TEXT

Here, write out the scriptural reference to the verse or verses you will read to begin your devotion. Do not write the words of the verses, but only the particular reference you will turn to in your Bible.

OBSERVATIONS

Here you will write the main observations you personally see from these verses that you would like to group to focus on. You may list these observations in the order they appear in the text or in order of importance. List each of these observations in your outline in as few words as possible.

- **Observation 1.** Write your observation, and also write a few buzz-words to help you remember any illustrations or stories about this observation that you may wish to share with the group.
- **Observation 2.** You may also list how this observation compares or is supported by other scriptures.
- **Observation 3.** You may have fewer than three or more than three observations.

APPLICATION

This is the heart of your message. Here, you will list and explain how the observations are relevant and applicable to all of us personally, to the group/team you are speaking to, or to the project your group is engaging in. You can use examples and stories for each point. Personal testimonies are also helpful. It can also be encouraging to share what one of your team members may have said or done that was consistent with this verse.

- **Application 1.** Don't make the applications too personal to you alone. Let them connect with others, too.
- **Application 2.** You may have fewer than two or three Applications or more than two or three, if you wish.
- **Application 3.** Your final Application point may, optionally, lead you to end the devotional message with a Call to Action (see below).

CALL TO ACTION AND/OR CLOSING PRAYER

Here is where you end your devotion. You may ask for a response from the audience, including an opportunity to receive the Lord, or you may simply close the meeting in prayer. For options to close your devotion with a call to action, see the advice points in Chapter 4. If you don't have a call to action, there is no need to add points to your outline here, so just use the heading "Closing Prayer."

Here is an example of a Biblical Text Devotion handwritten outline:

We Are Called to Fruitfulness

John 15:1-8 and 16-17

<u>Observations</u>

1. *Jesus has called us and appointed us to be fruitful (verses 2 and 16)*

2. *Jesus offers us the fullness of His joy (verse 11)*

3. *Jesus desires that our fruit and joy remain (verses 11 and 16)*

<u>Application</u>

1. *We must "abide" in Him.*

2. *We must love others. Lay down our lives for each other.*

3. *We must "go."*

Closing Prayer

TOPICAL DEVOTION FORMAT

The Topical Devotion format has 3 simple main parts (with sub-parts as shown below). You can add more parts to your devotion if you wish. However, this three-part structure is simple and adequate for a great devotional message:

- Topic
- Points (2-3 points, each with <u>scriptures</u> and <u>discussion</u>)
- Closing

Here is a more detailed description of what you will write under each of these headings and subheadings on your Topical Devotion outline. You can make an outline of your own using the topic you have chosen, or you may simply use one of the Topical Devotion Examples I have prepared in chapters 13-16 of this book.

TOPIC

State the topic you have chosen and describe why it is important. Tell the group that you will read scriptures and discuss each of the scriptures, as they apply to this topic.

POINT NO. 1

List the first point you wish to make about the topic.

- **<u>Scripture</u>:** Provide one or more scriptures that support this first point.
- **<u>Discussion</u>:** Discuss how this scripture applies to this first point. You can use personal examples and stories here. It is also encouraging to use positive examples from members of your group.

POINT NO. 2

List the second point you wish to make about the topic.

- **Scripture:** Provide one or more scriptures that support this second point.
- **Discussion:** Discuss how this scripture applies to this second point.

POINT NO. 3

List the third point you wish to make about the topic.

- **Scripture:** Provide one or more scriptures that support this third point.
- **Discussion:** Discuss how this scripture applies to this third point.

CALL TO ACTION AND/OR CLOSING PRAYER

Here is where you end your devotion. You may ask for a response from the audience, including an opportunity to receive the Lord, or you may simply close the meeting in prayer. For options to close your devotion with a call to action, see the advice points in Chapter 4. If you don't have a call to action, there is no need to add points to your outline here, so just use the heading "Closing Prayer."

Here is an example of a Topical Devotion handwritten outline:

Big Things Can Happen with Small Acts of Faith

1. *What May Seem Small Can Be Huge to The Lord.*
   Luke 21:1-4 and Mark 12:41-43
   Widow's mite (Bible mentions twice)

2. *He Multiplies What We Have to Give*
   Matthew 14:13-21
   Feeding of 5,000 (loaves and fishes)

3. *Our Obedience Is Valued*
   Matthew 20:6-11
   Parable of the Vineyard

Closing Prayer

For God has not given us a spirit of fear, but of power and of love and of a sound mind. Therefore, do not be ashamed of the testimony of our Lord, nor of me His prisoner, but share with me in the sufferings for the gospel according to the power of God. (II Timothy 2:7-8)

SHARING YOUR DEVOTION IS AN EXCITING TIME. IT IS NATURAL to be a bit nervous, but keep in mind that it is an honor that the Lord has chosen <u>you</u> to speak to His people. So, remember that what you are about to do is a joint work between you and the Holy Spirit. The Holy Spirit will take your words and bring life to them as you share them with His people. Be encouraged as you share, knowing that He is at work and He will use you.

"For it is God who works in you both to will and to do for His good pleasure." (Philippians 2:13)

BEFORE YOU START – RELAX

The first and most important part of sharing is to pray before you begin. Simply ask the group to focus on the Lord. Then, pray and ask the Lord to bless your words to share what is on His heart for each person in the room, and that He alone will get the glory and praise. It doesn't need to be a long prayer, but it is important to begin the message by personally asking the Lord to use you to speak His Word.

As you start, take a moment and look around at your audience, as they are looking at you. This will help you to look "outward" into their lives instead of focusing too intently on what you plan to share. It will also let them know you are intending to focus on them and their needs instead of just delivering your message. This can also help you tailor your delivery of the message in a way that will be more receptive by each of them. Usually, the more people who are in your audience, the more formal you will naturally tailor your delivery. The fewer the people, the more personal and intimate your delivery will be. Be careful not to make your delivery too formal, as doing so may make the audience feel "distanced" from you and less likely to hear and receive.

If you are nervous at any point in the process, take a few deep breaths and try be comfortable and confident.

BEGIN TO SHARE

To start, the first thing you will do is to tell the audience what your biblical text or your topic is. If you are delivering a

Biblical Text Devotion, you may ask the audience to turn to the verse in their Bibles so you can read them together. You should give them a few moments to flip through their Bibles to find the correct verse.

Next, read the verse(s) you have chosen. You may instead consider asking others to read the verse out loud to start the devotion. Usually, if there are fewer than three or four verses to read, you should be the one to read them. If there are more than three or four verses, you may ask one or more others to share in the reading.

Make sure you are speaking slowly so others can easily follow you, and speak loud enough for all others to hear you. I sometimes find that speaking slowly and loudly sets the stage in my own mind to project confidence, and it helps me feel more relaxed in the process.

CLOSING AND CALL TO ACTION

You may choose to close your devotion with a call to action, or you may simply close in prayer. To close your devotion with a call to action, you can do this in any manner that seems comfortable, and it will differ depending upon your message points. Some options include:

- You may ask them to take a moment to silently ponder the message and ask the Lord to reveal to them what He would personally be saying to them through it.
- You may ask for one or two volunteers to share a

testimony of their own concerning the things that you just shared.

- You may ask the group to break into groups of two or three to pray about the things they just heard or to lift up individual prayer requests. If you do this, you should tell them that they should only take a minute or two, and that you will keep time and announce when the prayer time is done.

- You may close by asking those who are not yet Christians to pray and receive the Lord into their hearts. You can do this during your closing by telling the audience that you will pray the "Prayer of Salvation" out loud. Then ask everyone to pray it with you out loud together, even if they are already Christians. At the end of this book, I have included a **Prayer of Salvation** that you can use. You can lead them through this prayer, sentence by sentence, so that everyone can repeat what you pray. As you read each sentence out loud, give them an opportunity to repeat that sentence out loud before you go to the next sentence. Afterward, be sure to acknowledge and follow up with each person who prayed this prayer with you for the first time! Welcome your new brothers and sisters into the Kingdom of God.

- It is not advisable to close the devotion by asking if the audience may have any questions about the subject that you just shared. If others have questions, they should ask you afterward.

IMPORTANT ADVICE

- Maintain eye-contact with your audience. It is okay to look at your notes, but it is best not to become overly-focused on your notes instead of also focusing on the audience. You can begin by looking directly at one or two people you feel comfortable with and talk to them as in a normal conversation. Then, move your eyes around the audience and focus on others, too. It is amazing how the Lord will use you in this. I find that, unknowingly, sometimes the Lord will have me look at particular ones while sharing a particular point because He meant that point for them personally.
- Don't speak in an "asking" tone. Sometimes those who are not used to speaking in public, or who may otherwise be shy, will deliver the devotional message as though they are asking the audience if this is okay. It is better to talk confidently with positive, uplifting voice inflections.
- Don't be afraid to let your personality show. This will make it easier for others to receive from you. It is better not to try and take on a different personality while sharing. For example, if you typically use humor in your interactions with others, you may interject humor into your

message. But if this is not your typical nature, it is wise not to try it in your message.

- Don't be too nervous. Most people are more concerned about themselves at the moment than about how you may seem to come across to them (and some of them are just glad that they are not the ones sharing). So, if you are overly nervous, you may take a moment to breathe and then speak a little bit louder. This helps to overcome the jitters.
- It is okay to engage the audience and make your devotion interactive, if want to. To make your message interactive, here are some questions you might consider asking:

"How many of you can relate to this point that I just shared?"
"What do you think this means?"
"What do you think should happen next?'"
"How should we properly respond to this?"

- Don't just read your devotion. Use your notes as a reminder of what to share next, not as a script to read. People will be more attentive and responsive to your message if it is more dynamic and personal, which creates an atmosphere of "in-the-moment interactiveness" with the message itself.
- Don't eat snacks or drink while sharing. This is too distracting.

- If you are nervous when you share, it is sometimes helpful to hold something in your hand, such as a pen, your notes, your Bible, or your cell phone. This helps to redirect your brain to also focus on something else, and it helps you to relax. But, be careful that you don't "fidget" with whatever you may be holding, as this can become distracting.

- If you are speaking to a bi-lingual group and your message must be translated, here are a few points to keep in mind:

- *You should prepare your message realizing that it will take twice as long for you to deliver it than usual. So, you may consider making fewer points to share and thus make it shorter.*

- *Talk slowly, and only speak one or two sentences at a time, to give the translator an opportunity to translate the message. Don't "talk over" the translator. Wait until he/she is done translating your last sentence before beginning a new one. It is often difficult to translate a message when you have to hear the next sentence at the same time as you are translating the first one.*

- *Use simple words that are more easily translated. Don't use idioms or words that have language-specific or culture-specific meanings.*

- Remember to smile and enjoy the process. This is a positive event, and if you smile often, others will feel more warmly receptive.

PART 2
TWELVE EXAMPLE DEVOTIONS YOU CAN USE IMMEDIATELY

If you choose to use any of these examples for your own devotional message, remember to write down the outline you will use in your own handwriting on a separate sheet of paper, folded into a one-half or one-fourth size sheet. You can also modify, shorten, or expand any of these, as you may wish.

For each of these devotions, I provide a sample of how your outline may look with your own handwritten notes. Then, I explain in more detail how you will deliver your message using this outline.

EXAMPLE FOR YOUR HANDWRITTEN OUTLINE

What Does God Require?

Micah 6:1-8

<u>*Observations*</u>

1. *God reminds His people of His own faithfulness to them. (verses 1-7)*

2. *The Lord shows us what He requires throughout His Word. (verse 8)*

3. *He requires us to "do justice," "love mercy," and "walk humbly with our God." (verse 8)*

<u>*Application*</u>

1. *Do Justly (give to others what is deserved). Care for poor, etc. (James 1:27)*

2. *Love Mercy (give to others what is not deserved). (Luke 6:36) (parable of two debtors – Matthew 18:21-35)*

3. *Walk Humbly with God (give God what He deserves - our heart) (Psalm 46:10)*

<u>*Closing Prayer*</u>

EXAMPLE MESSAGE USING THIS OUTLINE

BIBLE TEXT: MICAH 6:1-8

EXPLAIN THAT MICAH WAS A PROPHET AT THE TIME OF Samaria's fall to the Assyrians. His prophecies focused on Jerusalem and Samaria, and they were directed to social, political, and religious leaders who were often viewed as hypocritical. Then discuss that we all know the Bible tells us that we must live by faith. And we know that "faith without works is dead" (James 2:26). How then do we walk out of faith appropriately in our works and actions? What does the Bible tell us about what God requires of us?

OBSERVATIONS:

1. God reminds the people of His own faithfulness to them through the ages. He then instructs them that the formality of their "religious" practices do not satisfy Him (they don't reflect what He requires in their lives). (verses 1-7)
2. The Lord declares that He shows them (throughout His Word) what He actually requires, and He reminds them that they already know this. (verse 8)
3. God requires that His people (a) do justly, (b) love

mercy, and (c) walk humbly with our God. (verse 8)

APPLICATION:

1. Do Justly. (Give to others what is deserved.) This is a scripture theme throughout the Bible. (See Jeremiah 22:3). We are to care for those who are unable to care for themselves (James 1:2-27). This is an expression of our faith in God.

2. Love Mercy. (Give to others what is not deserved.) God extended mercy to us, through Christ, having made provision for our sins. He expects us to do the same for others (Luke 6:36). He did not give us what we deserved (death) (Romans 6:23) but instead gave us His salvation as a free gift (Ephesians 2:8). Read the parable of the two debtors (showing He requires us to act merciful to others who otherwise are deserving of our judgment (Matthew 18:21-35).

3. Walk Humbly With Our God. (Give God what He deserves – our heart.) God is more interested in our heart than in the vanity of empty deeds. He wants us to recognize His faithfulness (as He described in verses 1-7). He has done what we were unable to do. Read Psalm 46:10: "be still, and know that I am God..."

CLOSING:

Pray in closing that the Lord would help us to recognize where we may lack in our treatment of others and in humbly recognizing Him as God. Give an opportunity for your group to pray silently, and then after a few moments, you can close in prayer, exalting the Lord for His mercy and His greatness!

EXAMPLE FOR YOUR HANDWRITTEN OUTLINE

Exodus 3:1-7

Observations

1. God sees oppression/injustice and hears cries.

2. The place of revealing His plan was regarded as "Holy Ground." Moses was directed to remove his sandals.

Application

1. We should regard our work as holy. As Moses removed his sandals, we too should lay down defenses and be vulnerable with each other.

2. Be respectful at all times.

3. Walk carefully ("circumspectly").

4. Put on the armor of God (shod our feet with the gospel of peace).

Closing Prayer

EXAMPLE MESSAGE USING THIS OUTLINE

BIBLE TEXT: EXODUS 3:1-7

EXPLAIN THE BACKGROUND THAT MOSES HAD NOT YET BEEN called to lead the people out of Egypt. He was tending sheep for his father-in-law (doing his normal job of serving). Meanwhile, God's people in Israel had been suffering and had been crying out to God to deliver them. God revealed Himself to Moses in the burning bush, and gave Moses the call and direction to bring deliverance to the people.

OBSERVATIONS:

1. God sees oppression. He sees the difficulties and injustice that we and others experience. He has compassion and hears when His people cry out to Him for deliverance. (Perhaps God has heard the cries of the people and He has sent your mission team to help.)

2. When God revealed Himself to Moses, to bring deliverance to His people, God regarded the ground of His presence as Holy. God made clear to Moses to regard it as a holy moment and to take it seriously, by directing him to remove his sandals.

APPLICATION:

Ask for thoughts from the team as to what it might mean to regard this place/time as Holy Ground, too? Ask why Moses was commanded to remove his sandals.

1. We should regard our work with the Lord as holy ground, too. God told Moses to take off his shoes. We can use this as an example that we must also lay down our own defenses and comforts, and be vulnerable and transparent with each other.

2. We should be careful to act with respect at all times. When we meet with the Lord, He will instruct us. It is important for us to be respectful of direction and do what He says.

3. We should walk very carefully in all that we do (as Paul said, to "walk circumspectly" in Ephesians 5:15-16). Ask the group to envision what it means to walk carefully. Perhaps envision walking barefoot on an area with stones, trying to avoid them. Or, envision a soldier trying to be quiet and watchful. We should be equally as watchful to assure we step correctly when following God's plan for us to act and work for Him.

4. As we prepare to do His work, we should put on the "armor of God" as described in Ephesians 6:15, where he says to "shod our feet with the preparation of the gospel of peace" (Ephesians

6:15). Here, you can ask the group what this might mean, and encourage them to share their faith, both with their actions and their words.

CLOSING:

Pray that the Lord will visit with each team member and speak His direction about his/her role. Ask the Lord to help each walk carefully in the Lord's presence so that God's holiness may be revealed and revered by all.

EXAMPLE FOR YOUR HANDWRITTEN OUTLINE

John 15:1-8 and 16-17

Observations

1. Jesus has called us and appointed us to be fruitful. (verses 2 and 16)
2. Jesus offers us the fullness of His joy. (verse 11)
3. Jesus desires that our fruit and joy remain. (verses 11 and 16)

Application

1. We must "abide" in Him.
2. We must love others. Lay down our lives for each other.
3. We must "go."

Closing Prayer

EXAMPLE MESSAGE USING THIS OUTLINE

BIBLE TEXT: JOHN 15:1-8 AND 16-17

EXPLAIN THE CONTEXT THAT THIS WAS THE TIME OF JESUS' final instructions to His disciples before He was crucified. If we were to give final instructions to our family before we die, we would tell them the most intimate and important things. So, message can be considered vitally important direction and encouragement from the Lord, not only to His disciples but also to us.

OBSERVATIONS:

1. God has called us to fruitfulness (verses 8 and 16). Verse 16 shows us we are both "chosen" and "appointed' to produce fruit. We were created to be fruitful. Our fruitfulness is important to the Lord (verse 2 even tells us that He must prune us to produce more fruit).
2. Jesus offers us the fullness of His joy (verse 11). He tells us the importance of abiding in Him so that we will experience the fullness of His joy.
3. His desire is that both our fruit and our joy will remain. He wants us to be productive and our work to have a lasting effect, not temporary or in appearance only (verses 11 and 16).

APPLICATION:

1. What does it mean to be fruitful? Could it mean that we should multiply by sharing with others so that they may know Christ? Ask, what does it mean that we are to bear the "fruit of the spirit" (Galatians 5:22-23)? We must "abide" in Him. That is the only way to fruitfulness. Fruit doesn't just happen. Fruit must grow and ripen (this takes time and nourishment). A fruit tree doesn't just decide to produce fruit and then push it out. It must first let life flow through the branches, develop into a flower, and then the fruit begins to grow, and then it ripens. And our fruitfulness is important to the Lord (verse 2). You can then ask the group what it might mean to "abide" in Him. Examples are regular time with Him in prayer and reading His Word, meditating on Him and talking about Him redemptively, and praying with others.

2. We must love each other and lay down our lives for each other (verses 12-13). He made it a point to say that this was a commandment, not a suggestion. This is how we make Him known in the world (John 13:35). How do we do this? Perhaps give some examples of how you observed others in the group laying down their own interests to love and serve others.

3. We need to "go" (verse 16). We need to make deliberate steps of faith toward our appointment and calling to serve Him and to bear fruit (e.g., sharing our faith with others). ("Go into all the world and preach the gospel...." Mark 16:15). Encourage the group to step out in faith into those things they feel the Lord is putting on their heart to do.

CLOSING:

Break into groups of 3-4 to pray that each will abide with the Lord and have courage to step out in faith, and that we will experience the fullness of the fruit and His joy that remain.

EXAMPLE FOR YOUR HANDWRITTEN OUTLINE

Exodus 33:1-3 and 13-16

<u>Observations</u>

1. God desires to be with us and bless us.

2. God lifts His presence when we sin.

3. We can change God's mind through intercession and repentance.

<u>Application</u>

1. The attitude of heart is important to the Lord.

2. The presence of the Lord makes all the difference.

3. Worship the Lord alone. Seek His way and to know Him.

<u>Closing Prayer</u>

EXAMPLE MESSAGE USING THIS OUTLINE

BIBLE TEXT: EXODUS 33:1-3 AND 13-16

EXPLAIN THE BACKGROUND THAT THE PEOPLE OF ISRAEL HAD sinned. Moses had gone up to the mountain to meet with God, and they were afraid that Moses had forsaken them. So, they formed their own god by making a golden calf, and they worshipped it. Now, Moses came down the mountain and saw what they did, and God expressed to Moses that He was angered over their sin. Moses interceded on their behalf and asked the Lord to forgive them. God then sent them onward with the task He had previously commanded them – to proceed toward the promised land.

OBSERVATIONS:

1. God desires to go with His people and to bless them (verses 1-3). Although they sinned, God still fought on their behalf (He sent His Angel to fight and drive out their enemies in verse 2). And God sent them to continue their journey to the place of blessing in the promised land (verse 3).
2. God lifted His presence from the people because of their sin (in verse 3, God said, "for I will not go up in your midst").
3. Moses walked closely with the Lord, and when

Moses prayed for the people, God changed His mind (verse 17).

APPLICATION:

1. We can "go," and God will bless our work, but it's the attitude of our heart the Lord is more interested in. We need to stay in unity with Him and with each other. Even when we feel discouraged, we must not turn to idols (means of comfort and rest apart from the Lord).

2. As Moses recognized, it is the "presence" of God that makes the difference in what we do! In verse 15, Moses asked the Lord that unless His presence goes with them to please not send them. We should ask for His presence, stay in the presence of the Lord, and release His presence to others.

3. We must worship the Lord and seek His way. The turning point of Moses' dialog with the Lord was verse 13 when Moses said to the Lord, "Show me now <u>Your</u> way, that I may <u>know You</u> and that I might find grace in Your sight." We should always seek to conduct our lives "His" way, not our way, and always seek to "know" Him. When we do, He restores His favor in our lives (like the Lord restored the people of Israel back into His favor after Moses intervened).

CLOSING:

Pray for the Lord to allow His presence to go with you, and that He will reveal His way that we may know Him. Perhaps this is also a good time to ask the group to consider whether they may have resorted to seeking comfort in anything other than the Lord (which may be an idol in our lives). This would be an opportunity for them to repent of this, as Moses did on behalf of the people, to return to His presence and favor.

EXAMPLE FOR YOUR HANDWRITTEN OUTLINE

Joshua 6:1-15

Observations

1. *Jericho was a closed city.*

2. *Everyone worked together.*

3. *They all persevered.*

4. *They had to remain silent (commune with God).*

Application

1. The Lord will give His strategy and we must trust Him even if the plan doesn't seem logical.

2. When we don't see results, we should continue to persevere, and when we do, we will see that He was at work the whole time.

3. The Lord will keep His promise and bring victory.

Closing Prayer

EXAMPLE MESSAGE USING THIS OUTLINE

BIBLE TEXT: JOSHUA 6:1-15

EXPLAIN THE BACKGROUND: JOSHUA HAD LED THE ARMY INTO Canaan (the promised land). God parted the waters of the Jordan River for them to cross. The day before they entered Jericho, Joshua encountered a "Man" with a drawn sword who identified himself as the "Commander of the Army of the Lord" (presumably, an Old Testament encounter with Jesus). The Lord told Joshua that He has given the city of Jericho into his hand. This was a special time that God called His armies to work together to achieve victory.

OBSERVATIONS:

1. Jericho was a closed city. Verse 1 says that the city was "securely shut up because of the children of Israel; none went out, and none came in." Perhaps this is just like some places we may go with the gospel – they sometimes are not wishing or willing to receive it.
2. They all worked together. The entire army had to work together to follow the instructions to circle the city. Certain members of the group had specific responsibilities assigned to them (verses 4-5).

3. They all persevered. The battle strategy was unique. The very last day—when they all were probably the most tired—they had to exert the most commitment by walking around the city 7 times. When they completed this task, at the end of the seventh day, the walls came down. They were able to see that Lord had been at work the whole time—the walls came down by the sovereign work of the Lord!

4. They had to remain quiet the entire time (until the last day). This must have been difficult to do for 7 days. This probably allowed for a lot of time of personal reflection between each of them and the Lord.

APPLICATION:

1. The Lord will give us His strategy for His work, and we can trust Him and what He tells us to do. It may not always make sense, but we trust He has an eternal purpose in mind. Sometimes He asks us to do things because He is working within us (such as asking the army to remain silent probably was necessary for Him to do a work in each of them as He prepared them for the battle).

2. Although we do not see results immediately, if we trust His plan, His results will follow. We should persevere even if we seem we are doing the same

thing over-and-over with little or no results. The army of Israel must have felt that walking around the city 7 times had no consequence, but through their obedience to do it, God accomplished a major victory on their behalf.

3. God keeps His promise and will give victory!

CLOSING:

Pray for the team and for the project. Pray that God will give the team His work plan and battle plan. You may consider asking the group to pray silently and persistently for the project throughout the day, and at the end of the day, to come together for worship prayer as a group. You can end the prayer with shout – as the Lord instructed the army of Israel in verse 5.

EXAMPLE FOR YOUR HANDWRITTEN OUTLINE

John 19:28-31

<u>*Observations*</u>

1. *Ask the group, "What was finished?"*

2. *"It is finished" is the translation of the Greek word "Tetelestai" (meaning finality, like a mortgage payoff).*

3. *"Perfect tense" - it means finished in past, present, and future.*

<u>*Application*</u>

1. *Jesus' death was an act of finality for our salvation—past, present, future.*

2. *We can't earn it. What He did was sufficient.*

3. *His work is eternal; we can trust Him past, present, future.*

4. *We need to call on His name.*

<u>*Closing Prayer*</u>

EXAMPLE MESSAGE USING THIS OUTLINE

BIBLE TEXT: JOHN 19:28-31

EXPLAIN THE CONTEXT. THIS WAS THE TIME OF JESUS' crucifixion. It was after His life and ministry and work were complete. His suffering on the cross was now complete. His last words before He died were an exclamation that "it is finished." After He said these words, He released His spirit to God.

OBSERVATIONS:

1. Jesus didn't say "I" am finished, but "It" is finished. He was not announcing that He was done working. He continues to live and work even after His death and resurrection.
2. The phrase "it is finished" in Greek (Tetelestai) refers to the finality of a large event. It was not just finishing a task; it carries the nature of the finality of something that is important and impactful (like paying off a mortgage, etc.).
3. The phrase is in the "perfect tense," meaning that it is finished in past, present, and future.

APPLICATION:

1. When Jesus died on the cross, it was the "final" act of our redemption for our sins (past, present, and future). God is not limited to the construct of time. His work is eternal, and this was reflected in this final declaration of Jesus before His death. When He said it was finished, this meant that our salvation was accomplished once and for all.

2. We cannot earn our salvation and favor. It was a price that Jesus paid Himself on our behalf. We do not need to pick up where He left off and try to earn our favor with Him or our salvation. That would be impossible and we can spend our life in failure trying. We can only obtain salvation by trusting in Him for what He has already done— which was an act of finality with relevance in the past, present, and future. We can trust Him for our eternal salvation.

3. God's work is eternal and outside of our time boundaries. We can trust Him because He knows our past, present, and future (and has made provision for all of them).

4. His death and resurrection were sufficient for our salvation. We need to call upon His name to be saved because His work was complete and final.

CLOSING:

Invite those who have not given their hearts to the Lord to received Him. You can pray the Prayer of Salvation with them. Tell the group that you will pray the Prayer of Salvation out loud, sentence by sentence, and that the whole group together (even those who are already saved) should repeat each sentence out loud together.

EXAMPLE FOR YOUR HANDWRITTEN OUTLINE

Mark 3:1-6

<u>Observations</u>

1. *Jesus knew who was there (the man and the Pharisees).*

2. *Jesus required the man to take steps of faith toward Him.*

3. *The "religious" crowd did not accept what Jesus did.*

<u>Application</u>

1. *Identify our own shortcomings and needs, even if we feel vulnerable.*

2. *Take steps of faith to the Lord. This may include forgiveness, restoration of relationships, etc.*

3. *We should not allow ourselves to be distracted away from the Lord by others, regardless of who they are, even those who may be spiritually mature.*

<u>Closing Prayer</u>

EXAMPLE MESSAGE USING THIS OUTLINE

BIBLE TEXT: MARK 3:1-6

EXPLAIN THE CONTEXT THAT JESUS HAD CONTINUED HIS WORK village to village. The Pharisees were religious men who feared losing the respect of the people as the others looked to Jesus and not to them. So, the Pharisees continued to follow Jesus around to hopefully trap Him in His words or to find something in what He did in order to discredit Him. They were keener to find what they could use against Jesus than they were in the truth of who He really was.

OBSERVATIONS:

1. Jesus knew who was there at that meeting. He knew He was being watched, criticized, and judged by the Pharisees, but He also knew the man was there and had a need that He could meet. The man had a withered hand and it was him and his need that Jesus focused on as His first priority.

2. Jesus called on the man in need to take steps of faith. He first asked him to step forward, and then he asked him to stretch forth his withered hand. This must have been a vulnerable moment for the man. Can you imagine the moment if God

asked you to step forward with your very most vulnerable weakness? What would you do?

3. The "religious" crowd did not accept what Jesus did. They were not willing to accept the wonderful miracle that Jesus did for the man, but only how they could use it for their own purposes and try to bring disrepute to Jesus.

APPLICATION:

1. We need to realize and identify our own personal needs and where we may fall short (like the withered hand). What are the withered hands in our own lives? What are those things that are not whole, but only Jesus can fix? Call them out to the Lord. Even better, we can pray with each other (James 5:16 says to "confess your trespasses to one another, and pray for one another, that you may be healed"). We may feel vulnerable, or even embarrassed, but Jesus is here to heal and we need to reach out to Him while He is near.

2. We need to take steps of faith and "stretch" out to Him. We need to focus on Him as if He and we are the only ones in the room, and not regard the others. The man with the withered hand could have shirked back in fear as he saw the Pharisees, but instead he stepped forward in faith toward the Lord, publicly. Sometimes we need to take a

step forward to see healing in our life. This includes stepping forward to admit fault, or seeking to restore a relationship with others even if we are not at fault.

3. Although what we do is between us and the Lord, others may not accept it. Even those who may seem "religious" or more spiritual than us. We must carry on with our relationship with the Lord anyhow.

CLOSING:

Ask the team to take one or two minutes of time silently before the Lord and in their own hearts to identify needs they have that the Lord wishes to heal (like relationships, etc.). Then, afterwards, you may consider asking them to break into groups of 2-3 other people who they are comfortable with and ask for prayer for specific needs. Pray for each other.

EXAMPLE FOR YOUR HANDWRITTEN OUTLINE

Matthew 25:1-13

<u>Observations</u>

1. *All ten virgins awaited the Bridegroom's return.*

2. *Only half the virgins were prepared when He came.*

3. *The time came suddenly, when they were all asleep.*

<u>Application</u>

1. *Abide with the Lord and stay full of the oil of the Holy Spirit.*

2. *Don't lose the awareness of His coming. It is our own responsibility.*

3. *Be ready. At some point, it will be too late.*

<u>Closing Prayer</u>

EXAMPLE MESSAGE USING THIS OUTLINE

BIBLE TEXT: MATTHEW 25:1-13

EXPLAIN THAT THIS PARABLE OF THE WISE VIRGINS IS AN illustration of our preparing for the time of the Lord's coming, and that we should not be caught unprepared. In this parable, we may consider the Bridegroom to be Jesus, and that the entry of the Bridegroom is His coming to take us away to be with Him in eternity. We may consider the lamps to be our lives that we must prepare and keep full with the oil of the Holy Spirit so we can carry His light to the very end.

OBSERVATIONS:

1. All of the virgins were waiting and anticipated the return of the Bridegroom.
2. Only half of the virgins were wise and prepared sufficient oil for their lamps.
3. The time came suddenly when the Bridegroom entered (they had all fallen asleep). When the time came, there was no going back. Only those virgins who were prepared were able to go in with him to the wedding.

APPLICATION:

1. Abide with the Lord and let the Holy Spirit keep us full with His oil. We can only rely on Him for strength.
2. The busyness of our schedules and the surroundings can cause us to forget and "slumber." We can lose our awareness that Jesus is returning, and we can begin to rely on our own strength (and not His oil). It is our job to keep our lamps full of oil; it is not someone else's responsibility.
3. The point is to be ready. We don't know when His time will come, but when it does, many will miss it because they weren't ready. When it is too late, it is too late!

CLOSING:

Ask the group to evaluate their lives before the Lord. Have they been faithful to Him? Do they allow Him to refill their lamps to keep burning continually, or have they fallen asleep and allowed their lamps to grow dim? Give them a time to renew their relationship with the Lord. If there are those present who do not know the Lord, you can give them an opportunity to pray the Prayer of Salvation at the end of this book.

EXAMPLE FOR YOUR HANDWRITTEN OUTLINE

<u>*Topic*</u>: *Big Things Can Happen with Small Steps of Faith*

1: What May Seem Small, Can Be Huge to The Lord

- *Luke 21:1-4 and Mark 12:41-43*
- <u>*Discussion*</u>: *Widow's mite small/huge (Jesus mentioned it in scripture twice)*

2: He Multiplies What We Have to Give

- *Matthew 14:13-21*
- <u>*Discussion*</u>: *Feeding of the 5,000 (boy <u>gave</u> loaves and fishes)*

3: Our Obedience Is Valued

- *Matthew 20:6-11*
- <u>*Discussion*</u>: *Parable of the vineyard (those who worked last hour had same reward – valued the same)*

<u>*Closing Prayer*</u>

EXAMPLE MESSAGE USING THIS OUTLINE

TOPIC: BIG THINGS CAN HAPPEN WITH JUST SMALL STEPS OF FAITH

EXPLAIN THAT WE OFTEN COMPARE OURSELVES TO OTHERS. And we often feel like we have less, or sometimes more, to offer than others. How does the Lord view this? How does He view our work (whether large or small)? What does the Word of God tell us about what Jesus values the most?

POINT NO. 1: WHAT MAY SEEM SMALL, CAN BE HUGE TO THE LORD

- <u>Scripture</u>: Luke 21:1-4 and Mark 12:41-43 (widow's mite)
- <u>Discussion</u>: The widow's coins seemed small to others, but to the Lord it was so large that He put it into the scriptures twice! Jesus values our contribution individually (not by objective measure). If she had more, then He would have judged her by the larger portion (but she didn't have more, so He only judged her based upon her giving of what she had). See Luke 12:48, "to whom much is given, much will be required." We are all held responsible and rewarded for what we have and give.

POINT NO. 2: HE MULTIPLIES WHAT WE HAVE TO GIVE

- <u>Scripture</u>: Matthew 14:13-21 (feeding of the 5,000)
- <u>Discussion</u>: Jesus multiplies what we have to give, so that all can be blessed. All the boy had were a few loaves and fishes, but they were enough to feed the crowd. This can be compared with what we personally have to offer to the Lord, whether things, time, talents, or words. If we are willing to offer up what we have, He is able to use what we offer to accomplish way beyond what we had ever thought. Perhaps give an example of how this happened in your life, or with someone else you know (Ephesians 3:20).

POINT NO. 3: OUR OBEDIENCE IS VALUED

- <u>Scripture</u>: Matthew 20:6-9, 11 (parable of the vineyard)
- <u>Discussion</u>: He called laborers to help in the vineyard at all hours of the day. This can be compared to His calling us to work in His service at different times in our lives. Some He calls early in life, and some He calls later in life. But, in the end, the reward is the same. Even those who worked only one hour (at the end) were valued

the same as those who worked all day. He rewards our obedience, not our sacrifice.

CLOSING

Encourage the group that God sees what they contribute to His work. No matter how small it may seem to them, God sees it through a different lens. Pray for God to multiply what we have to offer so that He may use what we give for the blessings of others and for His glory.

EXAMPLE FOR YOUR HANDWRITTEN OUTLINE

<u>*Topic*</u>*: Keep Our Roots Strong*

1: What Happens Under the Surface Affects What Is Seen

- *Mark 11:12-25*
- <u>*Discussion*</u>*: Fig tree dried up at the roots*

2: God Makes Roots to Be Sensitive and to Bring New Life

- *Job 14:7-9*
- <u>*Discussion*</u>*: Roots grow toward water (water of the Word and the Holy Spirit)*

3: We Should Avoid Things That Are "Spiritual Poison"

- *Hebrews 12:12-15 and I Timothy 6:10*
- <u>*Discussion*</u>*: Do not allow "bitterness" to poison us or our relationships*

<u>*Closing Prayer*</u>

EXAMPLE MESSAGE USING THIS OUTLINE

TOPIC: ROOTS

OUR ROOTS IN THE LORD ARE IMPORTANT. THEY DETERMINE our strength to endure hardship and our ability to grow and to bear fruit. Roots of a tree usually grow three to five times as broad as the tree itself. If the roots are strong, the tree can survive storms. Similarly, if our roots are strong in the Lord, we can handle the storms of life. We must make sure we plant ourselves in an environment that is spiritually healthy so we can draw nutrients for heathy roots.

POINT NO. 1: WHAT HAPPENS UNDER THE SURFACE AFFECTS WHAT IS SEEN

- <u>Scripture</u>: Mark 11:12-25 (Jesus cursed the fig tree)
- <u>Discussion</u>: When He cursed the fig tree, it dried up at its roots. It did not dry up from the top down. It took time, but ultimately, it became visible and not reversible. We need to keep healthy roots and keep them nourished because our "unseen" roots will ultimately affect our visible life.

POINT NO. 2: GOD MAKES ROOTS TO BE SENSITIVE AND TO BRING NEW LIFE

- <u>Scripture</u>: Job 14:7-9
- <u>Discussion</u>: Roots grow toward water. They sense where the source of water is, and they grow that direction. Our lives are the same. We need to keep ourselves healthy by allowing our roots to grow toward His "spiritual" water. We should water our spirits by the Word of God and by the water of the Holy Spirit (by communing with Him). The fact that our roots in Christ will grow toward His water (when we allow them to) is symbolic of God's redemptive nature. Job 14:7-9 shows us that no matter how far we stray from the Lord, He can bring us back and give new life when we seek His water.

POINT NO. 3: WE SHOULD AVOID THINGS THAT ARE "SPIRITUAL POISON"

- <u>Scripture</u>: Hebrews 12:12-15 and I Timothy 6:10
- <u>Discussion</u>: Good relationships should include forgiveness to avoid a "root of bitterness," and we should avoid the "love" of money and material things.

CLOSING

Pray for the team to develop spiritual roots deep in the Lord that will grow healthy and strong to withstand the storms of life. Encourage the team that God is at work to strengthen them and lead their roots to water wherever they lack, provided we seek after Him.

EXAMPLE FOR YOUR HANDWRITTEN OUTLINE

<u>*Topic:*</u> *The Hallmark of our Discipleship*

1: Our Discipleship Is Evidenced by Our Love

- *John 13:35*
- <u>*Discussion:*</u> *Our testimony to the world matters; actions speak louder than words*

2: Love Is Revealed When We Lay Down Our Lives for Each Other

- *John 15:13*
- <u>*Discussion:*</u> *Love is revealed when we lay down our lives for each other (not vice-versa)*

3: The Greatest of These is Love

- *I Corinthians 13:1-7*
- <u>*Discussion:*</u> *The greatest of these is Love, because God is love and it reflects Him personally*

<u>*Closing Prayer*</u>

EXAMPLE MESSAGE USING THIS OUTLINE

TOPIC: THE HALLMARK OF OUR DISCIPLESHIP

INTRODUCE THE TOPIC BY EXPLAINING HOW A THERMOMETER measures the temperature of our air, and a barometer measures the pressure of the atmosphere. We know how to measure physical things, but how do we measure spiritual things? We often think of certain people as being more spiritual than others. But, how can we know this? What does the Word of God tell us about how the Lord measures our commitment to Him?

POINT NO. 1: OUR DISCIPLESHIP IS EVIDENCED BY
OUR LOVE

- <u>Scripture</u>: John 13:35
- <u>Discussion</u>: Our testimony to the world matters. Sometimes actions speak louder than words. The world is watching each of us, and they interpret what we say and what we do. The Lord measures our discipleship based upon our love for each other. The world measures us the same way. We need to be careful that our love shows through action, word, and kindness. This is how others know if we are followers of Jesus. And it is a good gauge for us, too. We can know if we are close

followers of the Lord if we love the ones He has put into our lives.

POINT NO. 2: LOVE IS REVEALED WHEN WE LAY DOWN OUR LIVES FOR EACH OTHER

- <u>Scripture</u>: John 15:13
- <u>Discussion</u>: Love is revealed through what we do for others. Sometimes we may look at this verse backward and think in our hearts that it means "no greater love has a man than that his friends will lay down their lives for him." But, that is not true (it is only what we may sometimes wish for, or we think is a sign that since we are loved by others, we must be spiritual). But, love is measured by us laying down our lives for others. You must measure this from yourself outward. Perhaps give examples of how you have observed a team member laying down their life for another. Or perhaps ask the team to tell examples they can think of. Ultimately, Jesus is the best example because, as stated in Romans 5:8, "God demonstrates His own love toward us, in that while we were still sinners, Christ died for us."

POINT NO. 3: THE GREATEST OF THESE IS LOVE

- Scripture: I Corinthians 13:1-7
- Discussion: There are many important fruits of the spirit, but the greatest is love. This is because God is Love and our love is a direct reflection of Him. ("We love Him because He first loved us." I John 4:19)

CLOSING

Pray that God will enable each of us to know and experience His unconditional love for us, and that we can express this love to each other. Help us to be mindful of the needs of others and give us the courage to lay down our lives for the benefit of our brothers and sisters (so that the world will see the Lord in this).

EXAMPLE FOR YOUR HANDWRITTEN OUTLINE

<u>**Topic**</u>*: How Are We Viewed?*

1: We are Salt and Light

- *Matthew 5:13-20*
- <u>*Discussion*</u>*: Salt seasons, preserves, and makes people thirsty; light allows you to see the way and avoid harms and pitfalls*

2: We are Epistles (Letters)

- *II Corinthians 3:1-6*
- <u>*Discussion*</u>*: Our lives are an open letter for others to read; if we know His love for us, others will read that and be drawn in, too*

3: We are Ambassadors

- *II Corinthians 5:20*
- <u>*Discussion*</u>*: As Ambassadors of the Kingdom of Heaven, we represent our King to those around us*

<u>*Closing Prayer*</u>

EXAMPLE MESSAGE USING THIS OUTLINE

TOPIC: HOW ARE WE VIEWED?

Explain that God has chosen to reveal Jesus to the world through us, His church. This may sometimes feel overwhelming, especially when we seem to struggle with so many things in our lives. Jesus encourages us in His Word by giving us illustrations of how He shows the world who He is through us. Here are some of those encouraging illustrations.

POINT NO. 1: WE ARE SALT AND LIGHT

- Scripture: Matthew 5:13-20
- Discussion: We are salt and light. Ask what it means to be salt, and what it means to be light. We are salt to the world. Food is often bland without salt, having no flavor. And salt is also used as a preservative. Salt also makes us thirsty. Each of these can be analogous of how we can have an impact on unbelievers around us. It is Christ in us that gives flavor to the world, and our presence can help make others thirsty for Him We are also light. Of course, without light we are unable to see our way in life. Light not only shows us the way, but it helps us to avoid

obstacles and harms by revealing the truth of what may be around us. Light reveals truth. Discuss what each of these may mean.

POINT NO. 2: WE ARE EPISTLES (LETTERS)

- <u>Scripture</u>: II Corinthians 3:1-6
- <u>Discussion</u>: Whether we like it not, and whether we know it or not, our lives are as an open written book (or "epistle", i.e., a letter) for others to read. What we say and do is a story of Christ to others. We should be mindful of what the chapters of the epistle will reveal. We should live our lives to reflect a love letter from the Lord to the world, so that when they see us, they "read" how much He loves them. As we recognize God's love for us, our lives reveal that love to others, and that draws them to Christ. ("...the goodness of God leads you to repentance." Romans 2:4)

POINT NO. 3: WE ARE AMBASSADORS

- <u>Scripture</u>: II Corinthians 5:20
- <u>Discussion</u>: We are ambassadors of Christ. Ambassadors represent the Government they are from to a foreign land, and the ambassador speaks on behalf of their own Government. So

too are we, His disciples. We are ambassadors of
Christ. We are representatives of the King (Jesus)
and the Kingdom of Heaven. What we say and do
may very well be interpreted as official words
spoken on behalf of the Lord. So, we need to be
sure that our words are always gracious and
"seasoned with salt" (Colossians 4:6). We need not
only to represent Him well, but also to advance
His heavenly policies of love and righteousness.

CLOSING

Pray and ask the Lord that may we reflect Him, represent
Him well, and have the impact on this world that He wishes
us to have.

Dear Jesus,

I come before You now because I need You and I desire to have a personal relationship with You. I know that I am a sinner and that I cannot save myself. I am ready for You to be my Savior and my Lord.

I thank You that You are God's Son. I thank You that You came into the world and led a sinless life. You bore my sins in Your body, You died on the cross, and God raised You up from the dead. I thank You that this was Your divine plan from the beginning.

I come to You now and ask You to please forgive me for all of my sins. Forgive me for living my life my own way. I ask You now to be Lord of my life, completely. I ask You to please come into my heart and make me Your child, so that I can live with You forever. I receive You now as my Savior and as the Lord of my life.

Thank You, Jesus, for being my Lord. Please teach me about You and teach me Your ways, and help me to live my life for You.

Amen.

ABOUT THE AUTHOR

MIKE KASTLE is a servant of the Lord called to minister to unreached people in closed countries. He currently resides both in the United States and in China. The nature of his work requires privacy for reasons of security, so the name Mike Kastle is a pseudonym so as to maintain anonymity. Mike's true identity is kept private for the time being.

www.ingramcontent.com/pod-product-compliance
Lightning Source LLC
Chambersburg PA
CBHW071549150726
48000CB00002B/984